Bryony

RHYME CRAFT

Devon

Edited By Donna Samworth

First published in Great Britain in 2018 by:

YoungWriters

Young Writers
Remus House
Coltsfoot Drive
Peterborough
PE2 9BF
Telephone: 01733 890066
Website: www.youngwriters.co.uk

Book Design by Ashley Janson

SB ISBN 978-1-78896-532-3
Printed and bound in the UK by BookPrintingUK
Website: www.bookprintinguk.com
YB0361E

FOREWORD

Young Writers was established in 1991, dedicated to encouraging reading and creative writing in young people. Our nationwide writing initiatives are designed to inspire ideas and give pupils the incentive to write, and in turn develop literacy skills and confidence, whilst participating in a fun, imaginative activity.

Few things are more encouraging for the aspiring writer than seeing their own work in print, so we are proud that our anthologies are able to give young authors this unique sense of confidence and pride in their abilities.

For our latest competition, Rhymecraft, primary school pupils were asked to enter a land of poetry where they used poetic techniques such as rhyme, simile and alliteration to bring their ideas to life. The result is an entertaining and imaginative anthology which will make a charming keepsake for years to come.

Each poem showcases the creativity and talent of these budding new writers as they learn the skills of writing, and we hope you are as entertained by them as we are.

CONTENTS

THE POEMS

Tra-La-La Land

Music, music in the air,
Music, music everywhere.
Toot, toot
The trumpets go,
Plinky plonk, plinky plonk
The pianos sing,
Strum, strum, strum
Go the guitars.

In the long nights, the notes shine,
The four beat moon glows,
The flute owls flap their wings,
The cat curls his tuba tail.

Music, music everywhere,
Music, music in the air.

Would you like to visit?

Ana Prynne (9)

Dino Land

A land of beasts and babies
Some volcanoes are active
And some are nowhere near to erupting
Omnivores eating everything in sight
Herbivores eating plants and roots
Carnivores eating diplodocus and brachiosaurus
The land is so, so, so grassy
With monkey puzzle trees.

Daniel (9)

Supercar Land

S upercar Land is the place where nobody gets out of their cars
U nlock your favourite supercar and live in it forever
P eople eat, sleep, drink and live in their cars
E veryone likes to do drifting and doughnuts in their cars
R oads get jammed up when there are traffic jams
C racking cars are lent to the fastest drivers
A ccidents and crashes normally happen when going fast
R apidly, come and visit this place where you can smoke your tyres.

Jake Nicks (8)
Bow Community Primary School, Bow

A Land Of Peace

A land of beauty and peace,
all wars have ceased.
All people get along
with background noises of birdsong.

Lavender fields blowing in the wind,
unspoilt and untrimmed,
an overwhelming feeling
that I'm not dreaming.

The sound of a bubbling stream,
the whole world is one team,
I wait with no fear,
I'm so happy here!

Lennon Chandler (9)
Bow Community Primary School, Bow

Weird World

My world is weird, but not dumb,
it is full of fun and don't forget the puns.

Sometimes boring, sometimes not,
but you love it a lot.

People walk upside-down,
but they do make sure you don't have a frown.

Weird dinosaurs lived at the time,
and for some reason, they loved eating lime!

Grace Baskerville (9)
Bow Community Primary School, Bow

Sports Land

S ports Land is loud,
P eople who win are proud,
O n the pitch, balls bounce beyond the lines,
R eferees blow whistles and make different signs,
T eams and individuals play all day and night,
S o why don't you catch the next flight? Come to
Sports Land!

Abigail Drake (8)
Bow Community Primary School, Bow

Sun Land

The Sun Land is shiny.
The Sun Land has always shone,
but it's gone for you and me
so it's gone for everyone.
Sun Land is hot and pretty,
it burns through you!

Maddie Drew (8)
Bow Community Primary School, Bow

Warrior Cats

W ith cats that speak, everything is not always sweet
A t dawn, having a feed, like performing a great deed
R unning at top speed
R ecognised at group gatherings
I magining not being in cages
O n the fallen trees, dancing in the leaves
R ipping at the flesh of meat

C urious cats never wandering into traps
A lways having strange names (like Firestar and Sandstorm)
T easing kits, having fun
S ometimes mean and sometimes fun.

Vicky Worth (9)
Bradford Primary School, Bradford

The World Of Trump

There once was a man called Trumpy,
who ruined a beautiful country,
he built a large wall,
and caused spirits to fall,
he indeed did make everyone grumpy.

The next thing he started was war,
the rest of the world asked, "What for?"
He did a big cough,
his fox wig fell off,
but his shenanigans started once more.

He called off his trip to the Queen,
'cause he thought English people were mean.
Britain won't be defeated,
by the president who tweeted,
has a more stupid leader been seen?

Henry Hassell (10)
Chagford CE Primary School, Chagford

Sporting Cheer

A world of sporting heroes,
red, blue, yellow, black and green.
An Olympic sign above my head,
in the cold, fresh breeze.

I see, I see a land of green,
leaves that make you jump so high,
food that makes you feel alive,
fresh water that makes you increase your stride.

I see, I see a swimming pool, pure and blue,
a running pitch which bounces too,
a tennis court that speaks the scores,
and a cricket pitch for all.

I see, I see a netball court,
with lights to play at night,
a surf beach with warm swells,
a football pitch with glistening grass.

I see, I see a place of friends and family,
everyone cheering and celebrating.

Red, blue, yellow, black and green,
a healthy land of happy sport.

Daisy Rowe (10)

Chagford CE Primary School, Chagford

Train Land

Trains can go anywhere,
up rocky mountains and high in the air.
Across sandy deserts and under the sea,
even in London, which is a big city!

Along the coastline, and through big tunnels,
from a long way away you can hear the train rumble,
on high cliffs and through green woods,
past long trains carrying lots of goods.

Over tall viaducts and beside raging rivers,
through thick snow which makes you shiver.
So you see how good trains are,
they are big and tough and they go very far!

Ben Waterman (10)
Chagford CE Primary School, Chagford

Home Of The Sweet

S weeties across every part of the land
W et, sticky rivers of Coke flush from end to end
E very corner of Sweetie Land is a sugary place to be
E ntire cities full of sugar, black rock and lime grass
T he children stuff their faces on the way to school
I n the sugar grain, people on the beach watch the cola ocean go by
E lderflower cordial is thrown in the air by fountains
S weetie Land is a magical place, where sugar is the base.

Toby Skilton (10)
Chagford CE Primary School, Chagford

The Land Of Football

F ields of green cover my land
O utside play is all that's planned
O pposing teams playing to win
T ime is of the essence when the whistle starts the play
B all skills are needed when playing on my green
A ll supporters are cheering on their teams
L ots of goals are needed to be the winning team
L iving for football, in my land of dreams.

Louis Mead-Goddard (10)
Chagford CE Primary School, Chagford

The Land Of The Sky

In the Land of the Sky
everybody can fly
upon futuristic drones.
They fly around the city,
their feathers are so pretty
with happiness never before known.

For the penguins of the sea
are soaring above me,
gliding with all the other birds.
They have such fun in the air,
no wonder people stare,
and everyone's lost for words.

Brendan O'Brien (10)
Chagford CE Primary School, Chagford

The Frozen World

In my frozen world
I live amongst the ice.
Paw prints in the snow,
I begin my daily quest
to find a lemming before my rest.

I journey swiftly, light on my feet,
trotting through the Arctic snow,
whiteness as far as the eye can see.
My radar ears twitching in the biting cold air,
I hear the lemming fidgeting in his icy-cold lair.

River Terry (10)
Chagford CE Primary School, Chagford

Candy Land

Candy Land has lots of nice sweets,
you can go for a walk and pick yummy treats.
The animals are big, fluffy and puffy,
do not eat them or you won't stay lucky.
Candy Land is the best place ever,
you can spend lots and lots of time together.
It's tasty, beautiful and colourful,
all the sugar makes people hop!

Mimi Barrau (10)
Chagford CE Primary School, Chagford

Christmas Cheers

Christmas lights hanging bright.
Christmas tree glitters like a light.
Santa flying in the sky,
in his sleigh, way up high.
Children playing in the snow,
with everyone they know.
Snowmen glisten in the sun
as the children run and run.
This is the time of year
for everyone to cheer.

Chloe Dennis (9)
Chagford CE Primary School, Chagford

Diamond City

In Diamond City, high above,
the stars are so pretty, shining with love.
A star sparkling and twinkling so bright,
lighting up the sky at night.
Quick, make a wish as you see one fly by,
shooting across the magical sky
as I watch the sky at night,
I wonder who is watching too?

Chloe Andrea Gardner (9)
Chagford CE Primary School, Chagford

Crazy Land

Dolphins in jelly,
Jellybeans as sand.
Rocks are marshmallows,
Unicorns in the sky.
Cotton as clouds,
This is the place I like to lie as I close my eyes.
Go to sleep and dream so sweet.

Leotie Howard-Vallely (10)
Chagford CE Primary School, Chagford

Music To My Ears

I hear beautiful music being played.
I see children reading notes.
I smell roses thrown before the choir.
I touch the keys on the piano.
I taste the excitement of the crowd.

Bryony Rose Griffiths (10)
Chagford CE Primary School, Chagford

Under The Sea

In Crystal Palace, mermaids dance like a singing star.
The palace is as clear as a crystal, and as cosy and pretty as could be.
If I was there, I would be dancing in the pretty palace.
The rumbling isles cloak the sea and eat the mangrove roots.
The ocean fairies like the dairy that they have for the feast.
The sweet wheat is made into crab bread in the lab.
The joyful rainbow makes the unicorn's sad dad joyful.
Finally, when I go there,
I will dig where the rainbow is and find treasure.

Miya Scarlett Passmore (9)
Dartmouth Academy, Dartmouth

Rainbow Kingdom

Every day I get up while eating with my father.
I get dressed, I look impressed, and drive on my way to school.
While I'm there, I find a bear and find out he's made of rainbows.
We find some old rats, in old, tiny hats, and find out they're from Brazil!
I met a guy called Joe, he stubbed his toe, and fell down the loo,
he fell down the loo, with a bowl of beef stew, and landed on a rainbow!

R ain is terrible, rainbows are better.
A re rainbows cool to you?
I love them so much!
N obody likes a storm.
B right band of colour.
O h rainbows are my favourite thing!
W ater droplets fall from the sky.
S unshine and rain is what you need.

Jay Greenhough (9)
Eggbuckland Vale Primary School, Eggbuckland

Dream Land

Dreams in a bottle, dreams in your head,
you dream while you lie or you dream in your bed.
We don't know where they come from
but we know they are there.
Bad or good, as long as you don't lose your hair!
But it's hard to get to sleep, so I count sheep,
but when I'm stuck in a deep, deep dream,
my mum is standing there, eating ice cream.

All types of dreams and all types of wonders,
they are in your head until lightning thunders,
but when I go to sleep my mum says,
"Don't let the bed bugs bite,"
so that's the end of my poem, goodnight.
Zzzzzz...

Lily McShane (10)
Eggbuckland Vale Primary School, Eggbuckland

Crazy Cat Land

C at fun, crazy catastrophe.
R eady for fun, you and me?
A wesome fun for everyone.
Z ebra stew for more than one.
Y et somehow I'm always hungry.

C ould anything here even scare me?
A mazing things happen here,
T oday, we can

L ie down, no fear.
A nytime, come down and see,
N othing scary to scare me.
D ay after day, fluffy fun for all.

F ood all day, no need to bawl!
U p down, all around,
N ever any need to frown!

Rocco Eric Riddick Woodhouse (9)
Eggbuckland Vale Primary School, Eggbuckland

Breakfast In A Mythical World

A man was walking and he fell in a hole,
that led him to Mythical Breakfast Land.

The Mythical Breakfast Land fairy,
gave the man a tour,
but when they were halfway,
the man said,
"How do you have so much meat?"
The fairy said, "You will see."
So everyone in Breakfast Land had a big feast,
and one of them said,
"Where is the man?"
"He is in your belly,"
said the godmother,
and they enjoyed the feast
and ate the meat,
for breakfast.

Kadie Hext (9)
Eggbuckland Vale Primary School, Eggbuckland

Candy Wonderland!

C an you resist the sweetness
A nd the flavour?
N ever can I resist the candy.
D o help yourself to the chocolate rivers!
Y ou can eat anything but people.

W eird land, all edible.
O h, what a place to be.
N ever not eating.
D ear oh dear!
E at up, as food always regenerates!
R egenerated food all around you
L and of wonders
A nd mysteries!
N o lying, just
D ive into honey pancakes!

Marley Andrews (9)
Eggbuckland Vale Primary School, Eggbuckland

Unicorn Land

U nicorn in your dream
N othing else like this
I n a wonderful world of candy colour
C andyfloss or candy cane, they all taste the same
O n a unicorn kind of day
R ainbow made of glitter
N othing else like this in unicorn land.

L ovely unicorns as pets, as sweet as can be
A nd if you see these unicorns, you will feel special
N obody knows what colour they are, except for you
D on't tell anybody the secret of Unicorn Land.

Millie Redmond (10)
Eggbuckland Vale Primary School, Eggbuckland

Cloud Land Up In The Sky

High, up high above the sky
is a land made of clouds.
If you laid on its fluffy surface
you would fall asleep,
or you could play with a cloud ball.
You may want to eat cloud ice cream.
You would be proud if you had your own spongy house.
You might see a cloud mouse.
In the middle, you could see a unicorn playing a fiddle.
Small, fat, big or skinny,
it's the perfect trip for you.
There's a lemonade fountain,
and a cloud mountain.
I am here,
are you?

Kieran Jack Brookes (10)
Eggbuckland Vale Primary School, Eggbuckland

Christmas Land

C hristmas is the best time of the year
H ead on the pillow when Santa comes here
R est your eyes and get to sleep
I s Santa going to come here? Don't take a peek!
S ome presents are small, some are tall
T ime to wake up, it's time to open some presents
M y gosh, there are lots of presents under the tree
A s quick as a flash, I go open presents
S leep time now, Christmas is gone, time to wait
for next year.

Hannah-Mai Gilbert (10)
Eggbuckland Vale Primary School, Eggbuckland

The Food Mood

If you step into my kitchen and blink,
you are stood in my land of food.
You don't fight with my food,
you just eat my food, day and night.
I know you like my stew,
Sue the cow even likes my stew.
When she moos,
you can eat my food,
and get into a good mood!
Once you eat my food,
you might need the loo.
If you want to stuff your face,
come to my place.
There's even soda,
that's been drunk by Yoda.

Amelia Martin (10)
Eggbuckland Vale Primary School, Eggbuckland

Pet Land

Do you have a pet, small or big?
Is it scaly, fluffy, fat, or like a pig?

My land is full of pets, ugly and cute,
are you thinking of an owl with a loud hoot?

A pet can be a dog or a little cat,
or an alpaca wearing a top hat!
A pet can be treasured and loved forever
if you're allergic to frogs, will you get one? Never!

You can walk a dog, not a cat,
you can hold them tight, but don't squish them flat!

Chloe Symons (10)
Eggbuckland Vale Primary School, Eggbuckland

Sweet City

In Sweet City, everything is pretty,
it's made up of dreams, so everyone beams.

Everything is grand, so come visit this land,
where you can stuff your face, but still win every race.

The candy will come in handy
(although you might get a sugar rush)
but it all tastes lush.

The trees are made of candyfloss
and the carpets are made of cheese, so please,
come to Sweet City, where everything is pretty.

Ethel Mawi (9)
Eggbuckland Vale Primary School, Eggbuckland

A Normal World

Normal and kind,
but very hard to find.
Peaceful and quiet,
but not for long.
If you hear the sound of a stampede,
screeching like ravens,
they need to feed.
Thirsty, they need to drink,
but not something you would think.
They attack at night when you're asleep,
no screams, just a lot of blood.
They wash it down with fresh mud.
So careful now, before you sleep,
because I hear them coming quickly.

Alice Lydia Dawe (10)
Eggbuckland Vale Primary School, Eggbuckland

Sweet Chocolate Candy

Everything in my world is chocolate candy,
I hear happy children racing around the chocolatey school,
I see squidgy candy trees in the forests that are ready to eat,
I hear people licking their lips outside in the playground,
I smell sweet candy schools in the villages,
I touch the creamy chocolate lake that melts in my hand,
I taste fluffy candyfloss clouds up in the sky with my tongue.
I love chocolate candy.

Eva Stephens-Watkins (10)
Eggbuckland Vale Primary School, Eggbuckland

Party All Night!

As you step with your feet,
over the sleet,
walk through the doors,
and you see great big walls
covered in candy,
so shimmering and bright.
Step on the dance floor
and boogie all night.
As you eat chocolate cake,
dance with your mate.
Have some fun
and it will all be great!
Parties are all you need,
so get up off your knees,
and you will see the magic flow.

Leah Jade Johns (9)
Eggbuckland Vale Primary School, Eggbuckland

Rainbow World

R idiculous rock candy
A mazing apple sherbets
I ncredible treats to eat
N ice knockout sour treats
B ig beautiful Breaks
O ozing caramel dripping down
W onderful waffles

W onderful willow treats
O riginal candies in the shop
R ainbow Skittles
L ovely strawberry laces
D reaming humans.

Jessica Noble (10)
Eggbuckland Vale Primary School, Eggbuckland

Candy Land

When you walk outside your chocolate house,
you will see a chocolate fountain and a white
chocolate mouse.
With candy canes as sticks,
and big lollipops that you can lick.

Gorgeous, gooey gummy bears,
skipping happily and fish free,
two other gummy bears getting married magically,
and three marvellous marshmallow people
standing with their daddy.

Olivia-Rose Harmer (9)
Eggbuckland Vale Primary School, Eggbuckland

Mountains

M y very cold home
O pens my heart to make me rhyme.
U p the ladder, I climb,
N ice to be up here again,
T o see the sunny sky.
A smiling child looks up at me,
I suddenly cry, "Hi!"
N ow I have someone to remember me by,
S o everyone smiles at me when I walk by.

Sophie Adams (10)
Eggbuckland Vale Primary School, Eggbuckland

Summertime

It's summertime
and I'm here to rhyme,
so sit on your bottoms
and have a good time.

I lay on the beach
and looked up high
and I saw the birds
way up in the sky.

I saw the sea splashing away,
I saw the tide,
coming out to the bay,
and as quick as I could,
I ran away.

Kelsey Ann Honey (9)
Eggbuckland Vale Primary School, Eggbuckland

Party In A Dream

Inside my world
you can do whatever.
Anything you want,
even change the weather.
Have a cup of cola,
play on a trampoline,
make sure you eat that Cadbury's,
before you have more dairy.
You'll always be happy,
not a single tear,
never too sad,
but you're too young to drink beer!

Cayden Harris (9)
Eggbuckland Vale Primary School, Eggbuckland

Fantasy Land

Every day in Fantasy Land...
I hear dolphins singing and splashing about,
I see happy, shiny, blue dolphins somersaulting in the luscious lake,
I smell magical mango wafting through the forest,
I taste the salty air from the sea,
I touch soft, warm sand between my toes.
I love the wild and that's just me!

Ella Drake (9)
Eggbuckland Vale Primary School, Eggbuckland

Dark Middle Earth

Dark Middle Earth,
the eye watching around.
All Orcs fighting.
Hobbits in their houses
picking some apples
till the Orcs strike.
All battle Hobbits run.
Well, Orcs take control.
Gandalf comes and takes half out,
one tries to get behind him,
and he says, "You shall not pass!"

Reece Jordan (10)
Eggbuckland Vale Primary School, Eggbuckland

Nightmare Land

This land is where your worst nightmares hide...
I hear the sound of a chainsaw close to my body.
I see half-dead skeletons stumbling towards me,
I smell gloopy goo oozing out of a zombie,
I feel a cold chill rushing through my bones,
I think I am in the presence of a ghost!
Sweat drips down my forehead!

Grace Williams (10)
Eggbuckland Vale Primary School, Eggbuckland

The Gummy Bear Fair

It's a nice sunny day,
I really want to play,
but look what's over there!
It's the gummy bear fair!
There are lots of them there,
some are big,
some are small,
some are thin,
some are tall,
some are red,
some are green,
this is the best thing I've ever seen.

Missy Morgan (9)
Eggbuckland Vale Primary School, Eggbuckland

Underwater Adventure

The bright blue water as glimmering as the sky,
Sticky starfish stuck to the rock,
The seaweed is swaying,
The seahorses are playing.
Divers discovering the golden treasure.
Turtles tumbling through the watery depths.
Pufferfish puffing like shiny blue balloons.

Isaac Noble (10)
Eggbuckland Vale Primary School, Eggbuckland

Tap, Tap, Tap In The Haunted House

Over, under, in the door,
step over the glass
on the floor.
Turn around,
what was that?
Something is going
tap, tap, tap.
Up the stairs,
through the door,
in the cupboard,
tap, tap, tap,
oh no... Not that!

Tia Shute (9)
Eggbuckland Vale Primary School, Eggbuckland

Boxing World!

Big boxing pads
All down the street.
A huge boxing ring
on the roof.

There are muscly instructors
and mats on the floor.
Gear for protection
and fighting in the ring.
Ding! Ding!
Watch out,
Don't get struck!

Summer Laycock (9)
Eggbuckland Vale Primary School, Eggbuckland

Cute Candy Land

Candy, candy, all you can eat,
so yummy, what a treat.
Lollipops, big and round,
with candy cane houses and lollipop houses,
edible grass and all that you can ask,
I bet you can't resist.
Come to cute Candy Land
and have a laugh.

Lucy Dawe (9)
Eggbuckland Vale Primary School, Eggbuckland

Under The Sea

The land under the sea is not like you or me.
It is such a wonderful place to be,
from the rainbow sand which is so very grand,
to the new species of sharks called Rainbow Jaws!
It likes to take a pause for afternoon tea,
it's really lovely.

Charlotte Fisher (9)
Eggbuckland Vale Primary School, Eggbuckland

Icy Snow

My land is made of icy snow,
a lovely place where I like to go.
There are icy things in the school
and little icebergs in the pool.
My land is getting icy and snowy.
My land is made of ice and snow,
it gave me frostbite on my toe.

Hammad Kobir (10)
Eggbuckland Vale Primary School, Eggbuckland

Winter Wonderland!

As you walk in the snow,
it reminds you of home,
so warm and cosy,
it makes you dozy.
You dream of cream,
as you get a cup,
and drink it all up
and fly high in the sky,
as you see snowmen dressed in white.

Sydney Drake (9)
Eggbuckland Vale Primary School, Eggbuckland

Candy Land

In Candy Land,
everything is banned
except for tasty treats
that you eat with your teeth.

There are no sticks,
it's all candy bricks,
come and visit this place,
where you can stuff your face...

Grace Tickner (9)

Eggbuckland Vale Primary School, Eggbuckland

Music Land!

M usic is my passion
U nbelievably cool, it's a fun place to be
S leeping in a piano hotel
I t can be a bit noisy, but so what?
C ome to this land, it will be a blast!

Toby Thomas Clevett (9)
Eggbuckland Vale Primary School, Eggbuckland

Breakfast Land

Breakfast, breakfast,
you're the best,
you start my morning,
whether it's hot or cold.
It's a nice day,
but if you don't have breakfast,
it's the end of the world!

Nathan Jake Todd (9)
Eggbuckland Vale Primary School, Eggbuckland

Halloween Land

Under the bed are hairy legs
Crawling up to me,
There are little kids screaming,
Calling to me.

I hear birds tweeting
But children still screaming,
I hear a stream tinkling.

Olivia Leigh (9)
Eggbuckland Vale Primary School, Eggbuckland

Scary Forests

F orever creepy forest
O ver the mountains
R emember, or not?
E vil vs good
S ilent but deadly
T eaching ugly things
S o watch out.

Millie Watkins (9)
Eggbuckland Vale Primary School, Eggbuckland

Lava Pit

Fierce and fiery
The lava pit burns and boils
People are nice
And play with blasters
Trying to beat each other
It's a fun place
If you don't get caught on fire!

Harrison Brooks (10)
Eggbuckland Vale Primary School, Eggbuckland

Overwatch Land

A land made out of junk
It is in Australia
A mean, destructive place
With bombs, mines and bear traps
Watch out for roadhogs and junk rats
They're wanted!

George White (9)
Eggbuckland Vale Primary School, Eggbuckland

Dinosaur Land

In Dinosaur Land, everything is bland.
Blood flies everywhere, from man.
The trees are black, the grass is red,
everywhere you go, you'll see death!

Dylan James Slater (9)
Eggbuckland Vale Primary School, Eggbuckland

Halloween Land

I heard bones rustling around
I see pumpkin houses
I smell oozing gloop
I touch red watery blood
I taste the smoky air.

Charlie Ellis-Martin (10)
Eggbuckland Vale Primary School, Eggbuckland

Black Spirits

The moon shines bright.
From the window of inquisitive children's bedrooms,
you can see, very faintly, in the distance,
a cave shaped like a skull.

Inhospitable accommodation for beasts of all ages,
fireflies lighting it up with a luminous glow.
Black spirits darting amongst stalactites and pillars of rock,
there are goths slinking in the corners, thinking deadly thoughts,
and vast dragons with teeth like the sharpest knives.
If one of them were to awake, it would be catastrophic.
Humans have been known to have wandered too near the cliff
and been devoured in under two seconds.

Scorching, ebony-black lava, bubbling in a cavernous oasis.
Even after you trek up the steep cliff face,
you would still fall into the pool to certain death.
Serpents slither across the jagged walls,
a foul odour of rotting fish filling the cavern.

We don't know that much about Skull Cave,
all we do know is that it makes shivers go down your spine,
and your blood run cold.

Freya Warren (9)
Kenn CE Primary School, Kennford

Ninja Land

Ninja Land is where it all began,
there was nothing except the greatest ninja ever.

In his life, he went through all the bad and good.
Ninjas from all over the world admired him.

Jumping mountains, climbing trees and saving people,
that was normal on his schedule.

And when his grandson was born
you should have seen the smile on his face,
the grandson was called Lenny.

"Lenny, you will grow up to be a great ninja like me,"
and what was said was said,
on Lenny's third birthday, he went to ninja school.

Now Lenny's been at ninja school for five years,
doing the best he can,
he's now in the ninja academy
with his new uniform, like a warrior.

Claudia Frost (9) & Sydnee
Kenn CE Primary School, Kennford

Death Desert

Nothing more dreadful than this,
All sense of hope has died,
A place beyond space and time,
No one would hear if you cried.

A despicable wasteland,
Desolate, despairingly bleak,
Horribly hostile,
The walking corpses, reek.

The sand is made of ashes,
Hideous zombies roam,
There's a grim oasis of blood,
This place could never be home.

An inhospitable desert,
Horribly eternal,
A place full of hate,
All future is just dismal.

Amaya Coral Blakesley (8)
Kenn CE Primary School, Kennford

Unicorn Land

U nicorn Land is a place to be happy,
N ice and calm and peaceful it is,
I t's incredibly pretty,
C arefully the unicorns jump over the rainbow,
O ver and over the rainbow they go,
R ed, orange, yellow, green, blue, indigo and violet,
N ight is coming so they all calm down,
S o do you want to come?

Abigail Smith (8)
Kenn CE Primary School, Kennford

Movie Star Planet

On this wonderful, fairy-tale planet,
lives a pretty little girl named Janet.
Her brand new movie,
is rated by the public, groovy!

In this particular city,
everything designed is pretty.
Everyone here has a pet,
and they all love to get wet.

We all live in a building,
made out of huge cameras filming.

Darina Petrova (9)
Kenn CE Primary School, Kennford

Snow And Ice

It was a cold and frosty Christmas evening,
it was silent in the house,
until the midnight bell rang and I heard a bang.
I thought it could be Father Christmas,
falling down the chimney,
so I went to take a quick look.
But then my dad shook
me, and said, "You're having a dream!"

Jessica Greeman (8)
Kenn CE Primary School, Kennford

Happy Land

Happy Land is wonderful
Amazing is Happy Land
People are so happy in Happy Land
Yippee, hooray! I love it
Love is all around
Amazing Happy Land
No rainstorms
Do you want to visit Happy Land?

Edie Gilchrist (5)
Kenn CE Primary School, Kennford

Millie's Magic World

From my window, I can see...
an eagle gushing through the sky like a waterfall,
some puppies which are very small,
the sun glistening like a ball of fire,
drifting up higher and higher.
Spaghetti tangled up like snakes,
clouds which are being jumped on by cakes.
Candy Land is over there, but you have to wear a band.

There is a cave with a unicorn, how cute!
Shrek, Donkey, and Puss in Boots are being chased by newts,
Shrek is like a grumpy dragon with hiccups.
Piggies playing with nappies on them,
flying horses with a magic hen.
I can hear a mermaid dancing with a hula hoop,
with a dog who is stuck in a bog.
Rabbits and horses playing and running about,
Ed Sheeran singing away.

There is a fountain that looks like a mountain,
exquisite fairies flying about,
and a parrot eating a sprout.

Millie Phipps (8)
Kingswear Primary School, Kingswear

The Icy And Diamond Mountains

Lynxes pouncing, hares running,
magic pugs riding on owls.
Wind swerving everywhere,
snow falling on trees and mountains.
The moon shining as bright as the sun,
big, fluffy unicorns dancing on rainbows.
Frozen waterfalls as cold as ice,
shining water as bright as the sky.
The moon as dark as night,
spotty lynxes as spotty as stars.
Polar bear cubs as white as snow,
shadowy forests as dark as black paint.
Icy oceans full of penguins,
candy canes as stripy as zebras.
Wind howling, making gentle music,
Arctic wolves climbing mountains and hunting.
Shining snowflakes as bright as shiny glass,
mountains made of clear diamonds.

Iris Wyman (6)
Kingswear Primary School, Kingswear

The Colourful World

I can see...
A magical portal red and green,
A floating, shouting cat,
A mystical mega-stone, green and blue,
a sleeping cat, orange and black.

A flying ship, white and black,
a big plane, cyan and pink,
an eagle gliding along the ozone,
a haunted house in the green forest,
a rabbit in the lap, green and red.

An orange cow on the road,
rides rainbow clouds into space!
My big house in a small street,
a dog on a log,
zero sun, just snow that's black and white.

Balazs Sipos (8)
Kingswear Primary School, Kingswear

My Imagination

Frozen snowmen,
Mermaids swimming in the lake,
Hot-air balloons floating in the air,
Wizards are blooming in the clouds,
their children rushing their words saying, "Fun, fun, fun!"
at the sight.
Run!

A castle as beautiful as a princess' home,
the princess' home so dazzling and bright,
shining hair glowing in the dark,
the king is fast asleep,
princess wakes him up with her hair,
wake up!

Summer Louisa Andrews (8)
Kingswear Primary School, Kingswear

Magic Wood

Red dragon zooming,
the yellow sun is bright,
the hill is bright red,
the fire is like hot lava.
The sky is as blue as the sea,
the witch is going on her broomstick.
I heard a bird roaring,
the lion is eating doughnuts,
the dragon sees a dog.
The elephant is drinking milk,
stars are coming up in the light,
dragon's friends eat food,
the forest is beautiful.

James Mason (9)
Kingswear Primary School, Kingswear

Wonder Land!

Fox dragons like eagles with boys on their backs.
Rainbow sharks swimming in the sky.
A friendly bear waving his walking stick.
The red arrows soaring through the sea.
Baby dragons running around
learning to breathe fire, wanting to fly higher.
A snake climbing trees,
it grows the more it eats,
like a plastic bag.

Oakley Honey (8)

Kingswear Primary School, Kingswear

The Water Land

The planet was as frozen as snow,
the magic mermaids go,
the sun was burning hot
and the land was shiny like a cloud.
Floating boats are frozen,
gushing pirates zooming through the air,
gigantic people crashing the boat,
wonderful garden of flowers that grow.

Nicole Lao (9)
Kingswear Primary School, Kingswear

The Portal

When I look through my window, I can see...
Knights guarding a castle against a fire-breathing army of dragons,
Spikes as sharp as poisonous needles,
Birds crashing into tree trunks,
A sun as hot as fire,
A purple portal to a different dimension.

Jowan Rickard (7) & Jude Skilton
Kingswear Primary School, Kingswear

The Wonder Land

Mind-blowing mountains growing,
waterfalls gushing through the blue air,
flowers floating in the sky,
bridges curved like a rainbow.
Flying pigs dance and sing in the air,
and forests grow in the water,
water flowing softly in the air.

Leland Dorling (8)
Kingswear Primary School, Kingswear

Beautiful Unicorns

Beautiful unicorns galloping through the breeze,
birds soaring through the trees,
stunning mermaids shimmering in the sun,
boats floating on the ocean.
Sheep talking to each other,
people walking their giraffes.

Macey Morse (7)

Kingswear Primary School, Kingswear

Crazy Land

Glowing lights, shining bright,
Super tight as a rope.
Dragons, bright like diamonds,
Glowing as bright as a light.
A dog flying as fast as a flash,
A cat swinging, going crazy.

Flynn Deville (8)
Kingswear Primary School, Kingswear

Cloud Land

From my window, I can see...
Magical wizards, terrifying witches,
And clouds as clever as men.
There are fairies on the ferry,
And skeletons playing 'it'.

Mackenzie Nettleton-Stokes (8)
Kingswear Primary School, Kingswear

The World In Union

Rugby players, big and strong,
listen to their fearsome song.

Haka calls the team together,
All Blacks wear the mighty feather.

Red rose for the English team,
unstoppable and almighty they do seem.

The yellow and green of Australia,
they don't like to lose - it's failure!

Powerful forwards, backs and props,
scrum-halves and flankers; the ultimate
Springboks.

Scotland with their blue and white thistle,
showing good sportsmanship 'til the final whistle.

The teams stand tall and grand,
in this united Rugby Land.

William Morris (10)
Payhembury CE Primary School, Payhembury

Magical Mountains

White walls tower of ice and snow,
individual flakes give a sparkly glow.

Is that a river? You can't be sure,
ice-trees like you've never seen before.

Never-ending blankets and peaks of white,
shimmering ice-crystals form at night.

A bitter wind sends a chill around;
howling, whistling, an eerie sound.

Snowfall dancing to the ground,
this magical kingdom will have you spellbound.

Tobias Morris (10)
Payhembury CE Primary School, Payhembury

Football

F ootball is fabulous, whatever the weather.
O n a field, in the rain,
O r on a beach in the sun.
T ottenham Hotspur beat them all, Harry Kane, the best of them all.
B ut when you're talking Barcelona, Lionel Messi knock them over.
A ll the players around the world, chasing the trophies made of gold.
L unging forward with boots in the air.
L ightning fast without a care.

Alfie Bold (9)
Payhembury CE Primary School, Payhembury

L.O.V.E.

L.O.V.E.
Chocolate fountains,
Sweetie mountains,
Heart balloons fly,
High in the sky,
Give me the key to L.O.V.E.

L.O.V.E.
Dreamy lakes,
Creamy cakes,
Music and laughter,
Happily ever after,
Give me the key to L.O.V.E.

L.O.V.E.
Black-nosed puppies,
Always lucky,
Friends hold hands,
Across golden sands,
Give me the key to L.O.V.E.

Madeleine Wooff (10)
Payhembury CE Primary School, Payhembury

The Land Of The End

Beckoning you to eternal sadness,
this land is dangerous and full of madness.
No sweet food at all,
only ghosts and ghouls,
where life's once upon a time is the end!

No sugar plums,
no Santa comes,
no happy faces
in any places.
As empty as hell,
with the stinkiest of smells,
this is the Land of The End.

Alice Millett (10)
Payhembury CE Primary School, Payhembury

Forest Changing Land

F orest Land is always changing
O n the ground and in the trees
R ed in autumn, green in spring, are the colours of the leaves
E nding in brown, they fall to the ground and rot
S eeds fall down to the ground
T hey scatter here and there
S ome get eaten, some will rot, some will grow next year

Rupert Hammond (11)
Payhembury CE Primary School, Payhembury

Chocolate Land

Caramel gates reveal an oozing chocolate reservoir.
The planet Mars Bars light the Milky Way like a car in the dark,
The chocolate factory spews milk as hot as an oven.
The dormant volcano fizzes popping candy as loud as an airliner.
Gummy worms burrow in the cake-filled mountain.
The hot chocolate rain excites young children,
The gingerbread houses are as resistant
As the chocolate hills surrounding the city!
Chocolate Land is amazing!

Oscar Belso (10)
Ratcliffe School, Dawlish

Food Land

I hear deep frying chicken and chips,
tasty, tasty around my lips.
I smell salt and yummy food,
It is very good.
I taste chips dipped into rich BBQ sauce.
I ate it on top whilst riding my horse.
I touch greasy fingers as I high five with my friends
In our secret dens.
I see French fry-shaped trees
With little burger bees.

Jake Gordon (10)
Ratcliffe School, Dawlish

Ice Land

The animals come in all shapes and sizes,
Some are big and some are as little as a twig.
Polar bears sleep in the woods, but they do fight and they do bite,
But don't be alarmed because they sleep until dawn.
The Arctic hares are like polar bears but
They always get ensnared and scared of the king of the Arctic hares.

Aidan Hole (11)
Ratcliffe School, Dawlish

Magic Land

M y land is magnificent.
A magical land.
G aming fun with the king and queen.
I love this magical land.
C urly, magical land, curl into a ball with fun and excitement.

Tyler Roberts (11)
Ratcliffe School, Dawlish

Candy Land

C ool Candy Land
A nice place to eat
N ougat sweets are chewy to eat
D rive down the candy town
Y ou will enjoy everything and have fun.

Mason Rybak (11)
Ratcliffe School, Dawlish

Chocolate Land

Dairy Milk is chocolate
Made from milk.
It is a little bit like eating silk.
Galaxy chocolate
From another galaxy.

Archie Blain (10)
Ratcliffe School, Dawlish

My Land

I have a land, I made by hand,
the sky was pink and the floor was blue,
rainbows ripple and animals adore.

Animals like unicorns,
nice and pretty.
Isles of pandas and bunnies,
my land had many things,
also, animals, cute and fluffy.
Little charms they are,
so cute and hyper.

Rainbows made of putty,
rain made of vanilla lemonade.
The king, I called Kade,
he dances and prances all around,
never ever being too proud.
It all sits on my bedroom wall,
like it would stand in an art hall.
Ideas for making my land better,
I wrote it all down in a letter.

Keira Hamill (9)
Redhills Community Primary School, Exeter

Imaginary Land

I see some food, I'm in the mood.
M an, I love the cotton candy, it reminds me of my friend, Mandy.
A chocolate cake, big mistake.
G ive me a pie and I will cry.
I hear music, it makes me groove.
N ow, I see the Halloween tea.
A magic land is never sad.
R eally full of love, and then you'll be glad.
Y ou can see the pretty tree.

L ove is good and it should be.
A n incredible day is never grey.
N o more snow makes you grow.
D on't sew here, it makes you grow old!

Lola Thomas (8)
Redhills Community Primary School, Exeter

Candy Land

I was walking down my street,
And I found some amazing sweets.
I picked them up and thought,
What a pleasant treat!
I popped one into my mouth,
Bam!
Without a doubt,
I was running about,
In a dino-infested Candy Land!
There were lots of gummy bears,
And wrappers with tears.
Dinos with candy canes for necks,
And Maoams worth hundreds of cheques!
Suddenly, a mini marshmallow was licking my face,
But when I woke up, there wasn't a trace,
Of all my dinosaur mates!

Izzy Adcock (10)
Redhills Community Primary School, Exeter

My Land Only

In my land, there are candy cane treats,
to others, they taste sour,
to me, they taste sweet.

There are lots of fuzzy animals playing in the grass,
I would love to play with them
but others would rather pass.

There's a river of coconut water running down the road,
I would sit and lap it up
while others would rather kiss a toad.

This is because it is my land,
mine and mine alone.
I have fun in my land, while everyone else is banned.

Lou-Lou Kane (10)
Redhills Community Primary School, Exeter

Candyland

Candyland is a place of joy,
Lots of sweets for girls and boys.

Chocolate waterfalls and marshmallow clouds,
You can hear them, they're really loud.

Edible doughnut bushes,
They whisper shushes.

Candy cane and lollipop trees,
They don't have leaves.

In Candyland, there isn't sadness,
Or any madness.

Sebastian Dan (9)
Redhills Community Primary School, Exeter

Rainbows

R ockets fly in the sky,
A nd think of all the fun you will have
I n this land. You will see little heart flowers,
N othing could be better,
B ut no bad people will come here,
O h no, they'll never go.
W ait here with us,
S tay here and you will be happy.

Caitlin Smith (10)
Redhills Community Primary School, Exeter

Candy Land

Candy Land is a place for joy,
Lots of sweets for girls and boys.
Chocolate monkeys swinging on vines,
Candyfloss trees all in a line.
Jelly beans jumping on a giant marshmallow,
Gummy unicorns that are yellow.
The wonderful world of candy,
Everyone will enjoy.

Fareefta Chowdhury (9)
Redhills Community Primary School, Exeter

Dream Land

A place you travel in your dreams,
A place of clouds,
As light as air,
A place you can be as thin as a hair,
Just think, and you'll travel there.

Shannon Mangan (10)
Redhills Community Primary School, Exeter

Candy Land Only!

C andy Land is full of candy,
A nd is delicious,
N ever going to be mouldy,
D elicious in every way,
Y ours forever.

Honey Kirkham (10)
Redhills Community Primary School, Exeter

Fantasy World

In Fantasy World where unicorns wander free;
there is chocolate bark on a lovely blossom tree.
Little elves and fairies who live in tiny toadstools
and every day they go to little, tiny schools.

There's a huge pinball sun with vibrant golden rays;
snow marshmallows with diamond-like forms fall in waves.
Dairy Milk rain nourishes the young blossom seeds:
popping candy hail is what everybody needs!

Silky, satin Malteser bunnies giving birth:
brittle lollipop trees sprouting out of the earth.
Graceful gummy flowers dance in the chilly breeze
and elegantly reach for tempting cookie leaves.

Unicorns have stables of luscious honeycomb,
their silver, pointed horns are tasty ice-cream cones.
Seeing glimmering glitter carpeting the ground -
you're sure to know these magical creatures are around.

Rhiannon Cooke
St Budeaux Foundation CE Junior School, St Budeaux

Unicorn Land

It's just so fun here, but be warned;
you might become a unicorn!
If you want something nice to eat,
Sweetie will make a unicorn treat:
sprinkled cookies or chocolate cake;
gingerbread men or ice cream with Flake.

Everyone's desperate to come here
because of the Queen's special prized deer!
Houses here are made of sweets.
There are unicorns here you'll love to meet.
If you're a child, you'll want to go
to perhaps meet Sparkle who has a foal.
But if you don't, it's really okay,
as there's another one whose name is Mae.
Wait!
There's so much to tell, here's one thing more...
Rainbow and Blossom will open the door.

Isla Mae McBride (8)
St Budeaux Foundation CE Junior School, St Budeaux

The Apocalypse

T ime is up. You must begin to fight...
H orrifying zombies have arrived!
E liminating all the humans that they find.

A ll are plotting to kill you.
P utrid, rancid-smelling.
O nly killed with a shot to the head.
C an you survive until the end?
A s deadly as a venomous snake
L urking in the darkness.
Y ou'd better run! You'd better hide!
P eople turning a disgusting green
S huffling across the blood-covered floor.
E ventually, you will be dead!

Lily-Mae Yeadon (10)
St Budeaux Foundation CE Junior School, St Budeaux

Lolly Land

Lolly Land is the place to be,
as you eat lollies for your tea!
Don't fret parents, you'll get some too;
you only have to lick your shoe,
as everything's made of lollies:
lolly trees and lolly dollies.
There's just one problem with this land -
you always have a sticky hand!

Lollies, lollies here and there,
in fact, they're everywhere!
Sugary flavours are so good;
they put you in a lovely mood.
The lollies here are so, so sweet:
they're even used to clean your feet!

This is my land - a land of joy;
joy for every girl and boy.

Ruby Hill (9)
St Budeaux Foundation CE Junior School, St Budeaux

Cheese Land

Cheese Land is the place to be:
When you get there you'll agree.
What you see is what you eat:
There's cheesy grass beneath your feet!
When you swim, you swim in cheese;
Most of the time, this is done with ease.
There are no trees here in Cheese Land,
Instead of these, there's stringy sand.
You can eat your house which is so, so nice.
However, there's a problem... mice!
They love the taste, it's really yummy,
They'll eat your table and even your money!
There's one last piece of crazy news -
Most cheese people eat their shoes!

Jessica Shaw (9)
St Budeaux Foundation CE Junior School, St Budeaux

Christmas Land

C hristmas puddings,
H appy days,
R unning outside to see new snow,
I cing Christmas cookies,
S inging Christmas carols,
T alking to Santa: "Ho, Ho, Ho."
M aking thoughtful gifts,
A dvent candles glowing,
S nowmen smiling in the wind.

L aughing while opening presents,
A ll families in colourful hats,
N aughty Elf on the Shelf,
D elicious, chocolate shaped like reindeer.

Sapphire James-Shannon (7)
St Budeaux Foundation CE Junior School, St Budeaux

Animal Land

A nimal Land is the place to be,
N ewts and narwhals licking your knee,
I nsects crawling and zebras trotting,
M onkeys and meerkats eat fruit which is rotting,
A lligators and elephants,
L ions, tigers and jaguars.

L emurs are never behind bars,
A nteaters, pandas, flamingos and giraffes,
N o animals here are ever banned,
D inosaurs still exist here in this land!

Lucas Sowden (9)
St Budeaux Foundation CE Junior School, St Budeaux

Food Land

F ood carpets, the edible, tasty floor.
O val olives glisten in the daylight.
O ranges and lemons hang from broccoli branches.
D elicious houses made of red Leicester cheese!

L uxurious pools filled with tropical blue soda.
A mber carrots which the peas think are lilos!
N aughty banana splits playing on sugary, lace swings.
D ecadent brownies float in scrumptious caramel ice cream.

Seren Mae Davis (8)
St Budeaux Foundation CE Junior School, St Budeaux

Sweet Land

Sweet Land is somewhere you can go.
Where tiny little bubbles blow.
Come along and stuff your face
With candyfloss that looks like lace.

Beware the colourful peppermints,
they fill your head with crazy things.
Sweet Land is such enormous fun,
with sweets that come from the golden sun.

Come with all your friends to play;
you'll never leave - you'll want to stay!

Courtney Ann Rick (8)
St Budeaux Foundation CE Junior School, St Budeaux

Sweetopia

Marshmallow trampolines.
A rainbow made of Skittles.
Houses made of gingerbread,
and lots of peanut brittle.

Happy faces all around,
a dull moment, never!
The stack of giant Oreos
Which doesn't fall down... ever.

The mountains made of ice cream,
and rivers made of milkshake.
If you go down the chocolate falls,
you'll end up in the 'Pit-of-Cake'!

Oliver Blewett (10)
St Budeaux Foundation CE Junior School, St Budeaux

Park Land

P ark Land is a place you can stay.
A place of magic and wonder.
R oundabouts make you laugh.
K ites that fly in the sky.

L ong slides which give you a thrill,
A nd swings that make you smile.
N ever lonely - you can play with your friends.
D ancing, exercising, having fun.

Isabella Trow (7)
St Budeaux Foundation CE Junior School, St Budeaux

Dark Land

'Twas the darkest hour;
not a speck of light.
No animals lurking -
what was wrong with the night?

Zombies rising up
to terrorise the town:
only one person remains
(with a very worried frown.)

The 'undead' crowding around him,
then... a pain in his brain!
What's going to happen next?
Will he ever breathe again?

Elliot Tucker (10)
St Budeaux Foundation CE Junior School, St Budeaux

Candy Surprise

Tasty treats in all shapes and sizes
in this magical land, there are many surprises.
Visit Lollipop Stop or Rhubarb River and float on
down in a candy boat.
Take a visit to meet Shoelaces Headcase,
he is tasty strawberry liquorice, all curled up
tightly,
but watch out, he is really mighty!
He likes to steal all your treats and gobble up all
the sweets.
Rainbow Skittles, helps you find your way,
to stay in this land and forget Torbay!
Eat what you like, ride a candy cane bike
or fly on a sherbet saucer, where Candy Land looks
smaller.
Way up high, you can eat some treats but watch
out
for the marshmallow clouds, you might meet!
Collect lots of goodies and make some new
friends,
because in Candy Land, the tasty fun never ends!

Ruby June Manley (9)
St Marychurch CE Primary & Nursery School, Torquay

Candy Land

Candy Land, where the houses are grand,
where the windows are wobbly
and the paths are all cobbly.
The trees are made of coffee
and its fruits are all toffee.
The bushes are marshmallows
and the jelly lakes are shallow.
The snakes are all gummy
and taste good in your tummy.
The chocolate cats are all black
and makes a nice, tasty snack.
But don't fall in the blackcurrant river,
it's so cold you will shiver.
Swimming in the sea so blue,
are gummy fish for you to chew.
On the land and all around
candy people can be found!
This land is amazing, fab and cool,
so come and visit, don't be a fool!

Reuben West (8)
St Marychurch CE Primary & Nursery School, Torquay

Magical Underwater Land

My land is underwater.
Everything is yummy.
Lovely ice cream gummy bears.
There's a castle under there.
Very good clothes to wear.
A magical speedboat to ride.
Not a dirty thing, not a crumb.
Very calm music everywhere.
Filled with pirate fish,
and a nice bedroom for the underwater king,
but his servants feed him with all the food.
Freshwater to drink.
Visit him at any time.
Enough money just for him.
You can just chill.
He's a cool fool.
It's as big as a house,
this calm, cool castle.

Devon Wilkinson (8)
St Marychurch CE Primary & Nursery School, Torquay

Food World

I can hear a blueberry juice river as watermelon boats go by.
I can see my juice carton house and the mashed potato clouds.
I can smell lots of different food smells.
I can taste candyfloss and candy cane trees.
I can touch the chocolate floor and also lovely meringue roundabouts.
I love it best in my world.

Abigail Scarlet Mealin (9)
St Marychurch CE Primary & Nursery School, Torquay

Candy Land Surprise

Gumdrops, lollipops and candy galore,
lots of sweets that make us want more.
It's now time for some candy fun.
At the swimming pool, we all have a chocolate bun.
People picking lollies and eating lots of candy,
you grab what you wish, which is very handy.

Leela Cartwright (8)
St Marychurch CE Primary & Nursery School, Torquay

Candy Land

C andy, candy,
A ll shapes and sizes,
N aughty but nice,
D elicious flavours,
Y ummy in your tummy.

L ush sweets to eat,
A ll to enjoy,
N o one can resist,
D on't eat too many.

Alicia-May Moon (9)
St Marychurch CE Primary & Nursery School, Torquay

Candy Town

Everything in Candy Town is made from candy,
I hear happy birds singing in the trees,
Candy factories chugging away,
people eating candy.
I see people unwrapping candy,
I see people building candy men,
I see birds flying down, trying to get candy.
I smell pots mixing and pans baking,
I smell new candies being tested,
I smell strawberries being mixed.
I touch candy cane pictures,
I touch candy men, they are freezing,
I touch beautiful statues.
I taste yummy candy cakes.
I taste yummy candy everywhere.
I taste delicious candy whiskers too!

Oliver Hywell Tobias Simpson (7)
St Peter's CE Junior School, Tavistock

Animal Land

In Animal Land,
everything is grand,
there are lots of animals as big and small as can be.
From the ones who eat meat,
to the ones who eat things off a tree.
It may be rainy and damp,
or as hot as a lamp.
There are gigantic giraffes too,
small cows who say, "Moo,"
also, there are jaguars with ginormous teeth.
For the rhinos and elephants, there's no thief,
There are lots of animals, as big and small as can be,
from the ones who eat meat,
to the ones who eat things off a tree.

Lauren Mya Walker (8)
St Peter's CE Junior School, Tavistock

Everything You Could Imagine

Golems roam in the biomes,
skeletons dance and party, also they are arty.
Houses like mansions,
mountains and snow, rivers flow.
Bird watching lodges in the trees,
animals and nature everywhere,
lakes for fishing, plates for dishing up food.
Portals to enter,
dragons to slay.
Pets to look after,
forests and friends to play,
rapids of lava to stay away.
Chests to find,
caves to discover,
plants to develop,
come and visit this wonderful place,
remember to bring a suitcase!

Sion Hathaway (8)
St Peter's CE Junior School, Tavistock

What Shall I See?

In this rainforest, what shall I see?
Beautiful animals, having their tea.
I might see an elephant, playing the trumpet,
or maybe a dinosaur, eating a crumpet.
Look over there, Mr Skunk testing Miss Rhino's horn,
but what's he doing with such a magical unicorn?
Wow! An otter having a barbecue,
it's as smoky as a cigarette.
OMG, there's a rabbit riding a bike,
and a lion playing the drums.
The drums are played as good as an elephant would.
A whole orchestra!

Bethany Carty (8)
St Peter's CE Junior School, Tavistock

Lovely City

In Lovely City,
everything's nice.
Everyone has a smile on their face,
the swings are lollipop sticks,
the rivers are half chocolate, half water.
The trees are leaves with candy canes on the top.
At the bottom of the river is flying dust.
All the animals love the humans.
The cement is caramel,
the bricks are jelly.
If you get bored, swim with the gummy snakes
in the chocolate river.
Come to this place to stuff your face.

Emma Lane (8)
St Peter's CE Junior School, Tavistock

Fluffy Land

F un would be like a roller coaster coming to the end of a whole new world.
L ots of cuddles coming to you and landing on massive marshmallows.
U tterly soft and comfy all around.
F luffy kittens, fluffy pets, even fluffy teddies that cuddle you.
F lavourful flavour in the rain and air all around you, I swear.
Y our fluffy favourites have come to town with happiness too.

Lola Adams (9)
St Peter's CE Junior School, Tavistock

A Magical Place

You have all seen lots of magical places except one.
I see trees made out of candy canes,
a house made of honey,
candy canes for trees,
colours as bright as the sun,
a rainbow running through the air.

I can hear a unicorn neighing,
the chimney puffing smoke,
the creaky hinges on the windows.

I feel happy,
I feel excited,
I feel joyful,
I feel jolly.

Lauren Molly Whitcher (7)
St Peter's CE Junior School, Tavistock

My Land

My land, my land, how pretty is it.
It's got all my friends living in it.
My land, my land how peaceful it is,
it's got everyone doing press ups in it.
My land, my land, it's got everyone eating jelly in it.

My friends are Evie, Sophie, Alba, Hazel, Bethany and Darcy.
Music makes me feel as happy as anything,
because in my land, music is always the best.

Maisy Peek (8)
St Peter's CE Junior School, Tavistock

Football Land

Football, football, you use your feet to kick a ball,
Goal, goal, that's what they say when you score a great goal.
Football, football, you use your feet to kick a ball.
I'm a Chelsea cheerer,
A Barcelona baller,
A moving Madrid.
I'm the best footballer around.
Football, football,
Did you know there's a Football Land?
Come if you want to play me.

Liam Jay Willson (8)
St Peter's CE Junior School, Tavistock

Book Land

B ook Land, it's a place to read.
O n a lovely hill is a book tree.
O n Book Meadow, where you can sit down,
K ind book fairies lead you to Book Cottage.

L ovely books, everywhere,
A nd the hill has unlimited books.
N ever boring, and sunny, it's the best place you can go.
D ream of lovely stories every night.

Amélie Travis (8)
St Peter's CE Junior School, Tavistock

Rugby Is The Game

Running and scoring,
tackling and kicking,
rugby is the game!
Scrums and swiping
out to the wing.
Rugby is the game, yeah!
Rugby is the game!
Making a maul
is the hardest of them all.
Rugby is the game!
Rugby is the game!
Getting knocked,
they will shout
rugby is the game!
The pitches are big,
the mud is thick,
rugby is the game.

Harry Witcher (8)
St Peter's CE Junior School, Tavistock

The Land Of Dinosaurs In 1999

Dinosaur Land is scary,
dinosaurs rule the Earth
from top to toe.
Dinosaur bones, lying on the ground.
Wriggling raptors flying everywhere,
dinosaurs eating meat and leaves.
The names are Apatosaurus,
Riley the raptor, Angry the axehead,
and Honkey the hammer.
Imagine dinosaurs ruling the Earth.
Volcanoes erupting,
lava running down the volcano.

Noah Durrant (8)
St Peter's CE Junior School, Tavistock

Food Land

In Food Land, everything is yummy,
chips in bread will make you stop dead!
But that's not all, if you start to yawn
it's probably because you've lived there since you were born!

It's no curse, you won't even need your purse!
There is a toaster, so there's no need to be a boaster,
because there's enough heat for everyone,
so enjoy!

Molly Anne Baker (8)
St Peter's CE Junior School, Tavistock

Ice And Snow Land

Ice and snow in all my land,
there is absolutely no sand.

Sparkling ice shining from the sun,
nice, deep snow in my land.
Oh no, I'm stuck in the snow!
Wow, I'm slipping on the ice.

I see lots of mountains up ahead,
you don't want to go to bed.
Sliding snow everywhere,
I'm going to slip, don't you dare!

Orla Rose White (8)
St Peter's CE Junior School, Tavistock

Melody Land

People are singing
with beautiful voices.
Extraordinary elephants,
terrific tortoises.
Musical melodies are filling the air,
as fast as an aeroplane zooming through the air.

Birds are singing a really sweet tune,
but the sun is humming along too!
The guitar forest does tune in quite a lot,
even though the strings are in a knot!

Hazel Stead (7)
St Peter's CE Junior School, Tavistock

Nature Land

N ever disrespect animals
A lways care and share
T rot on horses
U gly or not, you're allowed
R emember to get a picture
E very animal is here.

L ook around, see what you can find
A re you adored?
N ever hurt a creature,
D o play with the animals.

Seren Victoria Sulsh (9)
St Peter's CE Junior School, Tavistock

Candy Land

C andy Land, Candy Land,
A ll I need is this.
N ow it is here, all the candy is here,
D o I need more?
Y eah, it is all I need.

L uckily I'm here.
A pples are nothing but healthy!
N ow I need something,
D efinitely, candy, just because it is all mine now.

Izzie Gawman (8)
St Peter's CE Junior School, Tavistock

Candy Dreams

I n your candy dreams, you will imagine.
M y land is made out of candy dreams.
A ll the time you're there, you're happy.
G etting candy off candy trees.
I n the candy forests of candy trees.
N ext to clouds fogging near the floor.
E ach person turns to candy, hopping along.

Rose Pettit (9)
St Peter's CE Junior School, Tavistock

Fire And Water Land

F laming hot volcanoes
I gloos melt in seconds
R apids of lava
E verything is covered in fire.

W et people roam across the land
A nts are nowhere to be seen
T aps are the main thing here
E ven when the volcanoes are bursting
R unning with the water.

Noah Adams (9)
St Peter's CE Junior School, Tavistock

Animal Winter Wonderland

Snow is falling,
squirrels are storing,
for the wintertime.
Polar bears are skating,
round and round the ice.
But for me, the cold ice feels nice,
wolves and foxes jumping in the snow,
are they friend or foe?
Winter Wonderland,
Winter Wonderland,
where animals are playing,
everywhere you go.

Hannah Willis (9)
St Peter's CE Junior School, Tavistock

Have You Seen A Unicorn?

Have you seen a unicorn?
Neither you nor I, I know they're magic, right?
Rainbow tails, pink, blue and yellow glitter.
Glittery unicorn tails have glitter right?
Unicorns are real in our heads and daydreams
but when all of the girls' dream, night and day,
unicorns are really just fake.
Or are they?

Daisy Brown (7)
St Peter's CE Junior School, Tavistock

Nightmare

N ight-time is scary.
I ncredible, scary night.
G iants will get you at night.
H ugging, they won't bite... yes they will!
T arantulas are in your bed.
M ight they bite?
A bsolutely, yes.
R apidly biting.
E xecute, they will.

Jakob Moody (8)
St Peter's CE Junior School, Tavistock

Trampoline City

In Trampoline City, everything is pretty,
kids flying everywhere, nothing is a pity.
Jumping side to side through the city,
everything is fun when you hit your bum.
Jumping up and down is especially fun.
You can jump on the rooftops, jump on the floor.
You can do anything in Trampoline City.

Oscar Gascoigne (8)
St Peter's CE Junior School, Tavistock

Bow Land

B eautiful bows.
O h, how much colour!
W ow, how many wonderful bows?

L eaving this land would not be possible
A nd if you did, take a bow with you!
N ever forget the one and only Bow Land.
D eep under, you'll always know it's there.

Laura Such (9)
St Peter's CE Junior School, Tavistock

Mystic Magic

M y land is so mystical, as mystic as can be.
A land full of joy and what a lovely time.
G eniuses love their lands so much.
I just love it, it's so bizarre, I love my land.
C an I just not love it so much? I suppose as it is covered in spots!

Emily Mitcheson (8)
St Peter's CE Junior School, Tavistock

Land Of Epic

E verybody is welcome to use the cloud.
P arrots are welcome to charge your Internet iPhones.
I nternet storage is all free and no limit for stuff to save.
C omputer beds and breakfasts are more than seven pixels in price, hope you enjoy your visit!

Hazel Rich-Pearce (8)
St Peter's CE Junior School, Tavistock

Overlord World

Evil will rule.
Overlords will duel,
Like a tiger bonding with its pride,
All creatures will make these strides.

The light will be a veil until it fails.
One will prevail,
Dark destruction kills light,
But that's all right.

Oliver Reeves (8)
St Peter's CE Junior School, Tavistock

Drum World

D ude, are you ready?
R ock and roll will make you steady.
U pbeat drums will fill your mind,
M ummy will be left far behind,
S o come and see this land of rock, where all
you'll get is hip and hop!

Ethan Andrews (9)
St Peter's CE Junior School, Tavistock

Chelsea Land

Every day there is football in my land.
I hear people cheering for Chelsea,
I see people cheering for Chelsea.
I smell Chelsea hot chocolates.
I taste Chelsea hot chocolates.
I meet Chelsea players.
I love Chelsea.

Alfie Swinney (8)
St Peter's CE Junior School, Tavistock

Rock Star

Rock stars rocking, people partying,
I need a drum, not a plum, one hundred percent!
I went to go and see a rock star, rocking,
I am fine now, I partied at a party without stopping.
Popcorn, because I see popcorn popping!

Macy Pohill (8)
St Peter's CE Junior School, Tavistock

Candy Land

Fab Candy Land everywhere,
Knobbly knees, shaking, wanting;
I'm in Candy Land every day.
My world of candy is in every place,
A candy fight for everyone.
Land of candy eating.
Delicious popping Candy Land!

Jennifer Kingwell (9)
St Peter's CE Junior School, Tavistock

Football Fever

F ootball fever
O n the muddy pitch
O ver the crowd
T he fever is here
B attling the school
A round the stadium
L iving the dream
L iving the life.

Kieren McLaughlin (9)
St Peter's CE Junior School, Tavistock

Galaxy Land

Come, come and see Galaxy Land.
Stuff your face with chocolate.
Swim in the Galaxy lake of wonder
and never get sick.
You don't have to follow your parents,
you will love the yummy, brown chocolate.

Emily Miller (8)
St Peter's CE Junior School, Tavistock

The Beach Land

B each balls rolling across the sand,
E agles flying across the sky
A nd crabs pinching people's feet.
C reatures picking for food all year round,
H ot sun is coming out.

Jazmine Carpenter (8)
St Peter's CE Junior School, Tavistock

Birdy Birdy

B irdy flying through waving trees.
I hear birds singing like the sun.
R ude birdy eats blossoms.
D ark blue birdy catches rings.
Y oung, bright birdy plays with rocks.

Lilani Sky Peck (7)
St Peter's CE Junior School, Tavistock

Just Add Magic

M y land is magic
A unicorn and fairy, you will find
G reatness is in this land
I n a land like this, there's nothing to miss
C olour is the main part of our land.

Amelia Fox (8)
St Peter's CE Junior School, Tavistock

Dog World

There are no hogs in Dog World.
The bogs are soggy,
Everything's wet.
Try a bone in the shape of a cone.
Everything's so soggy and boggy.
The plants are all white
In Dog World.

Dylan Lacey (7)
St Peter's CE Junior School, Tavistock

Water Land

Water falling everywhere,
falling from the sky.
The sky is as blue
as a whale watching
whales swim by.
Good to see,
this is Water Land,
it is always good
to see.

Tanisha Jago (8)
St Peter's CE Junior School, Tavistock

Slime Land

In Slime Land,
there's edible slime
and slime gummy candy
that you can still eat and play with.
It's still fresh and stretchy,
if you keep it in a tub.

Shannon Maci Bolt (9)
St Peter's CE Junior School, Tavistock

What Candy Land Means To Me

C adbury yummy,
A nd it's in my tummy.
N o more healthy food,
D ude, why, Candy World is the best!
Y ummy world.

Oliver Lillicrap (9)
St Peter's CE Junior School, Tavistock

Snow Storm

Oh, I am the king of snowmen,
I've lived here for years and years.
I've never been slushy
or melted, or mushy,
or changed into a puddle of tears.

Oh, I am the king of snowmen,
I'm jolly and shiny and fat.
My home, small yet classy,
has skies, blue and glassy,
and snowstorms that swirl around my fluffy hat.

Oh, I am the king of snowmen,
I've never been known to complain,
but sometimes my galaxy rumbles,
oh terribly grumbles,
with striking earthquakes...
take cover! It's starting again!

Tianna-Rose Cox (7)
Woodfield Primary School, Whitleigh

Animal Party

Animal Island is exciting,
but there is lots of biting.
They giggle a lot
and jiggle a lot,
but the most important thing is at night.
They fight their prey.
There are lots of hills,
but no bills!
There are potions
and lotions,
and a big band.
When they go to a gig,
they dance a fun jig.

Miley Goad (7)
Woodfield Primary School, Whitleigh

This Is Our House

This is our house called Violet Vista,
and this is Susan, my horrible sister.
My mum and dad are very nice,
unlike my sister.
My brother is very mischievous and nosy,
but very nice and clumsy.
I've got two cats and one dog.
My dream house, the Violet Vista.

Madison Harriss (8)
Woodfield Primary School, Whitleigh

Animal Island

When it's time for stalking,
he stretches his muscles
and runs out and preys.
They roll up in balls
and roll around the island.
They only sleep in the day,
but not at night.
Would you like to live on this island?

Ebony Campbell (8)
Woodfield Primary School, Whitleigh

Spider Land

This is my spider,
he's fat and round,
when he gets taller and rounder,
he'll explode all over the place.

Layla Pinney (7)
Woodfield Primary School, Whitleigh

YOUNG WRITERS INFORMATION

We hope you have enjoyed reading this book – and that you will continue to in the coming years.

If you're a young writer who enjoys reading and creative writing, or the parent of an enthusiastic poet or story writer, do visit our website **www.youngwriters.co.uk**. Here you will find free competitions, workshops and games, as well as recommended reads, a poetry glossary and our blog.

If you would like to order further copies of this book, or any of our other titles, then please give us a call or visit **www.youngwriters.co.uk**.

Young Writers
Remus House
Coltsfoot Drive
Peterborough
PE2 9BF
(01733) 890066
info@youngwriters.co.uk